Charlie on Safari

written and illustrated by
Margaret Gratz

The Earth Lady
3675 Old Town Circle
Tupelo, MS 38804

ISBN 978-1-4507-3466-0

Book design by Maggie White, MAGraphics.

Printed in the USA through Four Colour Imports in Louisville, Kentucky.

For Charlie, Lucy, and Michael B.

Charlie lived in a yellow house
with green shutters

at No. 3 Bluebird Lane.

It was a quiet, peaceful neighborhood with nice people, friendly dogs,

and polite cats.

Charlie lived with his father and mother, little sister, Lucy,

baby brother, Michael B.,

and his loyal dog, BowWow.

Charlie loved his home at No. 3 Bluebird
Lane. He loved his family and his loyal dog,
BowWow, but Charlie longed for adventure.

Charlie wanted to go to Africa to see lions

and elephants

and giraffes

and zebras.

Charlie wanted to go on safari.

But Charlie could not travel far on his tricycle, and Charlie and Lucy had to be home every afternoon for "quiet time."

And BowWow was always homesick when he had to be boarded.

Where was Charlie to find adventure?

Charlie's father suggested that he look for adventure at No. 3 Bluebird Lane.

"Charlie, you and Lucy and BowWow could go on safari in your own backyard," he said. "If you are observant, you will discover that your backyard is truly a wild kingdom."

Charlie pondered on this for a little while, then decided that a backyard safari was a good idea.

So, Charlie grabbed his trusty binoculars, and Lucy grabbed her red satin evening bag, and BowWow barked with glee as they went out the back door in search of adventure.

The safari had begun.

The first stop was the bird feeder. Hiding behind a hydrangea bush, Charlie slowly raised his binoculars.

"Ah, fellow bird watchers," whispered Charlie, "I see a handsome red cardinal, a perky tufted titmouse, a contented goldfinch, and a chatty chickadee. Maybe someday, I will be a famous ornithologist."

"BowWow," shouted Lucy, "Look at the beautiful birds." BowWow wagged his tail and barked enthusiastically. But, alas, all of the birds flew away. Charlie just shook his head in dismay.

"Lucy, BowWow," scolded Charlie, "When you are on safari you must be quiet."

Back on the trail, the trio hiked past the bird bath.

"On to the backyard pond," said Charlie.
"Follow me. I am your fearless leader."

At the backyard pond, the adventure seekers spotted a dragonfly--a fierce predator--lurking at the water's edge.

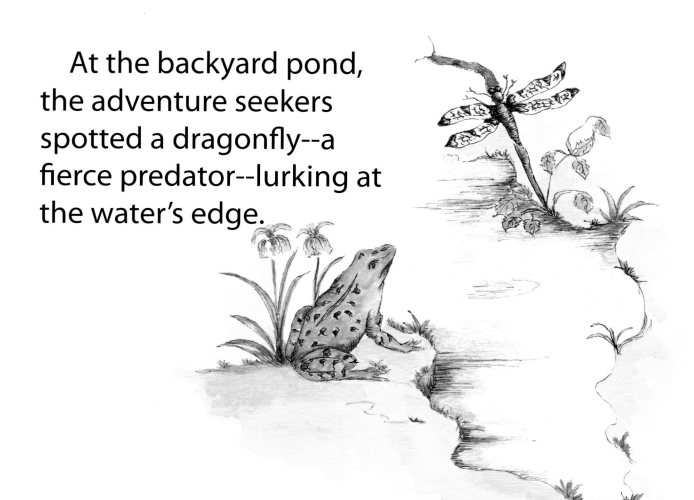

Nearby, a patient frog, an amphibian, sat waiting for a careless insect to fly his way. Across the pond, a curious turtle surveyed the scene.

BowWow barked at the turtle. "Don't bark, BowWow," scolded Lucy. "Sh! Be quiet, BowWow."

"Sh! Be quiet," said Charlie. But it was too late. The dragonfly flew to an overhanging branch. The turtle withdrew into his shell. "Ribbit, ribbit" said the frog and leaped into the pond.

Charlie just shook his head in dismay.

The safari continued. In single file, Charlie and Lucy and BowWow hiked past the daylilies to the patio where Charlie's mother had pots of herbs.

"Aha, I think we have a caterpillar eating the parsley. I believe this is the larva of the Order Lepidoptera. It is the exotic Eastern black swallowtail butterfly," said Charlie.

Lucy poked the caterpillar with her finger, and it stuck out its osmeterium, two orange horns. The caterpillar emitted a foul odor.

"Charlie, this caterpillar stinks," said Lucy as she turned up her nose. BowWow barked, but the caterpillar did not run away. It just kept right on eating the parsley.

Charlie just shook his head in dismay.

Moving right along, the safari headed for the flower garden. Butterflies were everywhere.

Perhaps Charlie did not have a tiger or a zebra in his backyard, but in the flower garden there was a tiger swallowtail butterfly and a zebra swallowtail butterfly.

There were other butterflies too--monarchs, gulf fritillaries, and yellow sulphurs.

Charlie and Lucy and BowWow laughed and chased butterflies, but the butterflies did not seem to mind all of the commotion. The flower garden and butterflies were so much fun, but there was more adventure ahead.

"This garden spider is very beneficial, and I do believe this is the largest spider I have ever seen," said Charlie.

Lucy really wanted to scream, and BowWow really wanted to bark, but Charlie was getting perturbed, so they tried to be brave and quiet.

Leaving the garden spider behind, they forged ahead to the zinnia patch, where Charlie found a green lynx spider.

"It may not be a wild lynx, but a lynx spider will do," said Charlie with glee. "This arachnid is called the lynx spider because it pounces on its prey like a cat."

"Charlie," said a wary Lucy, "BowWow and I do not like spiders. Let's look for something else."

"Okay," said Charlie. "But why don't we take a break?"

   Sitting on the bench by the hummingbird
feeders, Charlie and Lucy and BowWow ate
cookies that Lucy had brought along in her red
satin evening bag.

Overhead, ruby-throated hummingbirds flew in and out like daredevil pilots. Lucy did not scream, and BowWow, the loyal dog, did not bark. They just ducked every time a hummingbird flew by.

After the cookie break, the adventure continued. On they trekked to the vegetable patch.

"Oh, my! A rabbit is eating the lettuce," said Charlie. BowWow, the loyal dog, barked and chased the rabbit away.

"And there is a green snake!" screamed Lucy. And Lucy, with BowWow, the loyal dog, not far behind, ran all the way home. They had had enough adventure for one day.

Charlie did not have time to comment on the snake's beauty or explain to Lucy that the green snake was harmless. The green snake gave Charlie a puzzled look and slowly slithered away.

But every good safari must come to an end, so Charlie headed home for lunch and "quiet time."

When Charlie grows up, he may travel to faraway places and go on safari. But until then, Charlie can always find adventure in his own backyard behind the yellow house with green shutters at No. 3 Bluebird Lane.

The End